Hustle While You Wait

The Journey from Vision to Purpose-Driven Leadership

Kenneth E. LeGrand

TIA Publishing, LLC

Dedication

If you can't fly then run, if you can't run, then walk, if you can't walk, then crawl, but whatever you do, you have to keep moving forward.

— Dr. Martin Luther King, Jr.

This is a special dedication to my mother. When we used to talk—every night at 10:00 p.m.—we would always end our conversations like this: I would ask her, "Mama, did I tell you I love you today?" and she would respond, "Yes, darling. AND I LOVE YOU YESTERDAY, TODAY, TOMORROW, AND FOREVER AND EVER, AMEN. **UNIKUE** IS THE WORD, AND THAT IS WHO YOU ARE, SO DON'T YOU FORGET IT BECAUSE I WON'T." Well, Mama. I have never forgotten, and I know you are always with me.

To my mother, Corina, now resting in Heaven. You taught me that people are real. They cry, they bleed, they feel. And no matter how they treat you, you reminded me that my place on this Earth is to take care of them, help them, and pray for them … no matter what.

Your compassion was fierce. Your faith … unshakable. Your love … unconditional.

Now, though your voice has gone silent here on Earth, I still hear you in every act of kindness I extend, in every prayer I whisper on someone else's behalf, and in every moment I choose grace over judgment. You gave me the strength to feel, the courage to forgive, and the wisdom to serve with humility.

Mama, because of you, I love louder. I care deeper. I give more. And even in your absence, you remain the heartbeat of everything I strive to be.

Thank you, Mama. Heaven holds you now, but your legacy lives boldly in me. I love you yesterday, today, tomorrow, and forever and ever, AMEN!

Author's Note

My mother used to look at me and say, "Boy, you're UNIKUE." She spelled it her own way and said it like a promise, not a compliment. At the time, I didn't understand how much power was in that word. But years later, I realized she wasn't just naming me—she was calling out my purpose.

There's an entire chapter later in this book devoted to that word, and what it's come to mean in my life and leadership. But I mention it here because everything that follows— every lesson, every hustle, every wait—was rooted in what she saw before I ever could.

Contents

Prologue

For I know the plans I have for you declares the Lord, plans to prosper you and not to harm you, plans to give you hope and a future.

—Jeremiah 29:11 (NIV)

The dream is free, but the Hustle is sold separately!

As I reflect on the journey that led to this book, I am reminded of the countless moments where patience and perseverance seemed like distant virtues. In a world that often demands immediate results, the concept of waiting can feel like an eternity. Yet, it is precisely during these periods of pause that we discover our greatest opportunities for growth and innovation.

Hustle While You Wait was born out of my own experiences with uncertainty and the realization that even in stillness, there is always room for action. This book is a testament to the power of turning waiting into a catalyst for progress. Through personal stories, strategic intuitions, and real-world advice, I aim to inspire readers to transform their downtime into a springboard for success.

In the journey of life, success is not just about reaching the finish line but about how aggressively and faithfully you run the race. *Hustle While You Wait* is a call to action—to keep pushing, striving, and grinding even when the outcome is not yet clear. I have proven that I have run the good race by embracing every challenge with determination and resilience and refusing to be idle in moments of waiting. This hustle is the proof of my commitment, the evidence that I am not just waiting for success—I am working for it, every single day. This serves as a reminder that the race is won by those who keep moving, no matter how long the wait. We just have to keep going. What I have learned in my life is that your pace doesn't disqualify you—your persistence secures the promise.

And if you're wondering where my hustle began, let me take you back. It was around 1974, in 4th grade. My dad asked me what I wanted to be or do when I grew up. In my very small town of Rockingham, NC, the big businesses were the CSX railroad, the hosiery mill plant (ALEO), and the chicken plant (PERDUE). All I could think about was making a lot of money, and I didn't think I could do that in my hometown. At that time, I can remember that many people were talking about the computer age. Sounded good to me, so I said, I want to be a "computer person." Heck, I did not know the right terminology back then. After all, I was only nine years old, so I had a long way to go. How was this going to happen? What did I have to do? When was this going to happen, and where? There were no answers for me at that time, but one thing was for sure: It wasn't going to be presto and happen overnight. It would take some time, but more importantly, it was going to be a process.

It was then that I had to realize it was not going to happen by my merely saying it, but that it would take steps for me to realize this vision, dream, future. Those steps would consist of school (middle and high) and then college. I could not wait for something to happen in order to get where I wanted to be, I had to move—Hustle. My dad would remind me, "Ken, even when hustling while you wait, you still have to wait on the results of your hustle." That made a lot of sense. You see, we do what we have to do now, so we can do what we want to do later. Unfortunately, some people just want to be a part of the moment. I call that the "duck mentality," which you will read more about in the coming chapters. Hard work can be time-consuming and very tiring, and requires not only patience, but also perseverance. Just because you don't see it doesn't mean it isn't there.

Your breakthrough is in your progress! Many people want the end result only if it's smooth sailing. They see your results, what they deem as your successes, those material assets, those tangible things. They see your house, they see your cars, they know that you travel (to them, quite frequently). They see that you have the "black" credit card. They don't see the discipline—the sleep I skipped, the things I gave up, the miles I traveled alone. They rarely ask, "What did it take for you to get where you are?" Now that's the million-dollar question! Where did you start? What sacrifices did you have to make? What were your priorities? Did you have to leave anything or any friends behind? These are the questions that are not asked.

I am hopeful this book brings you as much joy in reading it as it did for me in writing it. This book has been years in the making. Not because I stopped, but because I kept going. Life made me grow, fall, rise, and learn through it all. And through it all, I never stopped moving. That's why it bears the name *Hustle While You Wait!*

To every mentor who offered wisdom, to every friend who believed, to every family member who held me up—I am hopeful you realize that this is your fingerprint on my journey. This work is more than pages; it is a testimony. A collection of lessons carved from the labor, and proof that purpose doesn't pause. As you turn these pages, I invite you to walk with me—and embrace the truth that waiting is not wasting. Every moment—even the quiet ones—holds potential. Let us redefine what it means to WAIT. Let us rediscover the HUSTLE within. Because purpose doesn't pause. And neither should you.

Chapter 1

The Making of UNIKUE

Before I was born the Lord called me; from my mother's womb he has spoken my name.

— Isaiah 49:1

S ome moments don't need a stage, a spotlight, or a crowd to shape you. They happen in kitchens, on porches, or in quiet moments that you don't even realize are etching something permanent into your soul. For me, one of those moments came every time my mother looked at me and said,

"Boy, you're UNIKUE."

She didn't just say it—she declared it. She spelled it her way, emphasized every syllable, and said it like she knew something I hadn't fully caught up to yet. At the time, I'd smile, shrug it off, or roll my eyes like kids do when parents say things they don't fully understand. But deep down, those words stuck.

She spoke identity over me before I had the language to claim it. And now, looking back over nearly four decades of service, leadership, triumphs, setbacks, and growth—I realize that "UNIKUE" wasn't just a compliment. It was a calling (Jeremiah 1:5).

UNIKUE: MORE THAN A WORD

My mother's declaration became a quiet compass. In rooms where I was the only one who looked like me, in roles where the title didn't match the impact, in moments when doubt whispered loud—"UNIKUE" reminded me: I didn't have to fit a mold. I was built to shape one.

Years later, I took that word and gave it structure—not to limit its meaning, but to help me carry it intentionally. For me, UNIKUE became:

> **U—Understanding:** The beginning of wisdom. Leadership requires awareness.
>
> **N—Nurture:** Growth doesn't happen by accident; it's cultivated.
>
> **I—Integrity:** Integrity sustains influence long after charisma fades (Proverbs 11:3).
>
> **K—Knowledge:** The fuel for growth.
>
> **U—Unwavering Purpose:** Your compass through uncertainty.
>
> **E—Excellence:** Not perfection, but consistency in pursuit (Colossians 3:23–24).

PASSING THE GIFT FORWARD

This chapter isn't just about a word my mother gave me. It's about what I want to give to you. Somewhere along your journey, someone saw something in you—maybe they spoke it, maybe they didn't. But you were designed UNIKUE, too. Not to blend in. Not to shrink. But to bring something to this world that only you can bring.

Take a moment and reflect:

- What makes you UNIKUE?
- What truths have been spoken over you that you may have forgotten?
- What's waiting to be unleashed when you finally stop apologizing for who you are?

Write it down. Claim it. Own it.

MY MOTHER SPOKE IT. I LIVE IT.

My mother didn't give me a blueprint. She gave me a belief. And that belief carried me through boardrooms, deployments, late nights, hard choices, and seasons of waiting. She saw something in me long before I saw it in myself. She named it. She spoke it. And over time, I learned to live it.

My mother spoke UNIKUE over me. Today, I speak it over you. Because being UNIKUE isn't just about standing out —it's about standing in who you are. Unapologetically. Boldly.

With purpose and legacy in your stride.

The UNIKUE Framework

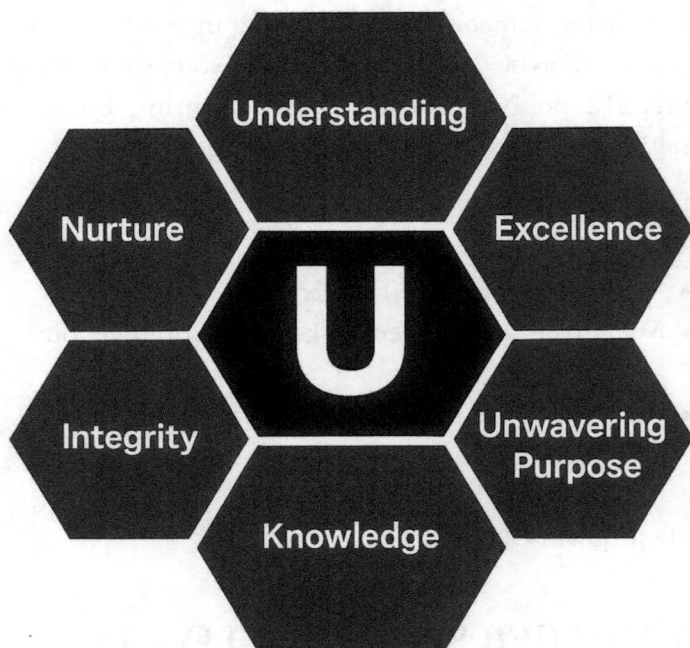

Figure 1. **The UNIKUE Framework**: *Six pillars surrounding the individual (**U**). A visual model of holistic leadership and growth.*

At the heart of this framework lies a simple but powerful truth: Progress doesn't start with systems—it starts with self. The "U" at the center represents you—the individual who chooses growth, integrity, and purpose, even when no one's watching. Every pillar radiates outward, showing that authentic leadership and progress flow from the inside out.

- **Understanding:** The beginning of wisdom.
  Leadership requires awareness—of self, of others,

and of the environment. Understanding bridges the gap between intention and impact. It reminds us that empathy and clarity must guide every decision.

- **Nurture:** Growth doesn't happen by accident; it's cultivated. Nurture represents investment—in people, in purpose, and in progress. Leaders who nurture others don't just build teams; they build trust and transformation.

- **Integrity:** The non-negotiable. Integrity sustains influence long after charisma fades. It's the invisible force that keeps your words, actions, and values aligned—even when the spotlight moves elsewhere.

- **Knowledge:** The fuel for growth. Knowledge isn't just about what you learn, but how you apply it. It means staying curious, adaptable, and humble enough to evolve. The best leaders are lifelong learners.

- **Unwavering Purpose:** Your compass through uncertainty. Purpose gives meaning to motion—it keeps your "why" intact when the "how" gets hard. It's the conviction that anchors your actions.

- **Excellence:** Not perfection, but consistency in pursuit. Excellence is the visible result of the other five pillars. It's what happens when understanding, nurture, integrity, knowledge, and purpose come together in alignment.

MEANING IN MOTION

The UNIKUE Framework is meant to remind you that true progress is all-inclusive. It's not about chasing status or applause—it's about building sustainable growth that's integral to who you are.

It's a leadership philosophy.

It's a life framework.

Chapter 2

Intentional Neglect

Therefore, to him that knoweth to do good, and doeth it not, to him it is sin.

—James 4:17

ACCOUNTABILITY

Intentional neglect is not just about what we forget; it's about what—or who—we choose to ignore. There are moments in leadership when supervisors are given the opportunity to do right—not as a favor, not for applause, but simply because it has been earned, not out of convenience or comfort, but out of conviction. And yet, they choose silence. They choose to look away. They choose intentional neglect.

Let's be clear: This isn't about guilt. This is a call to awareness—to truth and to responsibility. Because the most damaging neglect is rarely accidental. It's a decision to avoid what's uncomfortable, even when the right thing is well within reach.

In leadership studies, this is called passive avoidance behavior—when decision-makers sidestep accountability by doing nothing. Harvard research shows that inaction can erode trust faster than mistakes, because people remember when you didn't show up.

Leadership isn't about being perfect. It's about being accountable—choosing principle over popularity and legacy over convenience. Silence in the face of potential isn't humility—it's neglect dressed up as professionalism.

THEY SAW ME, BUT CHOSE NOT TO SEE ME

I wasn't invisible. I was intentionally ignored—on purpose.

I remember joining the agency nearly four decades ago, filled with ambition and ready to lead. I asked a simple question: "What would it take to become a senior leader?"

They told me I needed more education beyond my bachelor's degree. Easy. I already held a BS in Computer Science from North Carolina A&T State University, one of the most prestigious HBCUs in the nation. I also had a master's degree from Bowie State University in Management Information Systems.

Still, I was told my degrees didn't carry "currency." Translation? They wanted me to attend a "majority" institution. That's when I decided to do more. I enrolled at the Naval War College in Newport, Rhode Island.

Graduated as one of two civilians in a class of over 300 Naval Officers.

Still—not enough.

Then came the bar: "Manage at least 50 people." Check. I'd already led over 100 as Assistant Dean at a federal university serving the intelligence community.

Still—not enough.

Next? "Do a Permanent Change of Station (PCS) or a deployment—prove you can lead beyond the flagpole." So, I did both. I uprooted my family to serve overseas. I deployed for six months, leading both civilian and military personnel abroad.

And still—not enough.

Neglect never broke me—it refined me. This is what I call hustling through the silence. There was no fanfare. No applause. Just the weight of being intentionally overlooked, and the will to keep showing up anyway.

HUSTLING THROUGH THE SILENCE

I didn't stop moving. I didn't stop growing. I didn't stop leading. At first, intentional neglect was what I endured. But over time, it became what I mastered. I learned to intentionally neglect the noise, the doubt, the subtle dismissals. I let go of the need for approval. I ignored the politics, the backroom whispers, the gatekeepers.

Greg McKeown calls this Essentialism—the disciplined

pursuit of less but better. I just called it survival with strategy.

And in that quiet season, my growth took root. Because leadership isn't about being liked. It's about being loyal to something higher than applause. John Maxwell once said, "A leader who knows the way, goes the way, and shows the way." But sometimes, showing the way means walking alone first.

Real leadership doesn't come with theme music. It comes with awkward silences, hard conversations, and moments where you think, "Did I really sign up for this?" Spoiler alert: Yes, you did.

And if you're called to lead, you have to own it. Most won't. But the few who do? They build legacy.

THIS CHAPTER ISN'T A SHORTCUT— IT'S A MIRROR

No. This chapter won't give you "Three Easy Steps to Promotion." What it will give you is a mirror to reflect, confront, and recommit. Because the real win isn't in the title. It's in the truth—the kind you live when the easy way whispers your name ... and you still choose integrity.

KENNISM: "At first, intentional neglect was what I endured—being overlooked, underestimated, and undervalued. But in time, it became my power. I learned to neglect the nonsense, the noise, and the need for approval. And in that sacred silence I grew." They ignored the seed— but they could never stop the root.

Chapter 3

The Duck Mentality—Calm Above, Hustling Below

Do not be anxious about anything, but in every situation, by prayer and petition, with thanksgiving, present your requests to God. And the peace of God, which transcends all understanding, will guard your hearts and your minds in Christ Jesus.

— Philippians 4:6–7

Negativity

"I let that slide off like water off a duck's back. I don't soak in the nonsense—I stay focused on the mission."

Ever heard of the "duck mentality"? It's not about waddling around quacking for breadcrumbs (though, let's be honest, free snacks are always a plus). No, the duck mentality is about one thing: mastering the art of appearing composed while hustling like mad beneath the surface.

People often want your glide, but not your grind. They admire your calm but don't consider the cost of your composure. They see the results—position, poise, presence —but they don't see the sacrifices. The late nights. The stress. The second-guessing. The spiritual conversations with yourself in the mirror that no one ever hears.

WANT THE SMOOTH? LEARN ABOUT THE STRUGGLE

Let me be clear: People want what you have—but only when it looks good on you. They want your glow, but not your hustle. They want your shine, but not your storms. They didn't see you navigating waves, wind, and rain, because they were too busy judging how your feathers still looked good wet.

Here's the truth: Most folks only see the highlight reel of your journey. The promotion. The applause. But they didn't stay up with you during the breakdowns. They weren't there when you were swimming against the current with a smile on your face and a storm in your spirit.

The question is, "What did I do to even realize or put myself in a position for a promotion?" Late nights at the job, doing the extra stuff that others did not want or desire to do. The degree. Yes, I had a BS degree when I came into the agency, but I immediately went back and got an MS degree, on what was called the 20/20 program—I went to work 20 hours a week and school 20 hours a week. Talk about time management and priorities! And how about taking a position in beautiful Hawaii, but instead of golfing and beach time, I decided to attend the Naval War College for one year. Continuing to hustle, because I knew what I was doing today was only going to prepare me for tomorrow.

What they miss is that under every composed stride is the hustle beneath the surface—that part of you that never stops paddling.

BENEATH THE CALM: EMOTIONAL DISCIPLINE, NOT DENIAL

Don't confuse composure with lack of emotion. Oh, we feel. Deeply. But we choose to master our reaction. That's strength. That's not hiding—it's control. Emotional discipline is leadership. Leadership isn't about being cold. It's about staying clear. And clarity is born from being able to hold your peace in the middle of chaos.

There were days when you wanted to scream. Times when you were judged, misunderstood, underestimated—but you smiled anyway. That's duck mentality. That's grace in motion.

And let's be honest: Sometimes the paddling feels endless. You're tired. You're overlooked. You want to give up. But your forward momentum doesn't require their approval— just your persistence.

GLIDE WITH GRACE, PADDLE WITH PURPOSE

I learned to let others think it was easy. I even let them assume, in some cases, that I was naturally gifted. That's fine. Because I knew better. I knew that underneath the still surface, there was a story—one of discipline, faith, sweat, setbacks, and silent breakthroughs.

Sometimes being a leader means learning how to put in work without groaning. Hustle without highlighting. Succeed without needing a standing ovation. And, like ducks, I always strive to move through life with a calm head and determined feet.

So yes, I often smiled on the surface. Stayed poise. But I was never ashamed of the work below. That's why I embraced my inner duck. Glided when I could, paddled when I had to, and was never ashamed of the effort it took to stay afloat. Life isn't about looking perfectly composed all the time; it's about staying in the game, the hustle, even when the water gets choppy. And whenever I felt overwhelmed, I had to remember: The pond is big enough for all of us, and every duck—no matter how cool they looked on top—is working just as hard to keep moving forward.

Don't envy the glide if you don't respect the paddle. Before you wish for someone's grace, ask yourself if you're ready for their sacrifice. Because while I made it look smooth, trust me—I was paddling with all I had. Not to impress, but to stay afloat and faithful to the call on my life.

The Duck Mentality—
Calm Above, Hustling Below

Above the Waterline
Poise
Composure
Grace
Confidence

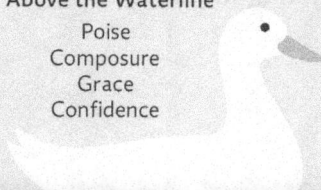

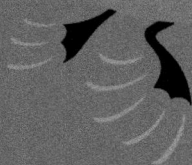

Below the Waterline
Hustle
Grit
Preparation
Persistence

Leadership often looks calm on the surface, but greatness is always working beneath the waterline.

The moral? Don't judge someone's journey by their surface-level serenity. For every person who seems to have it all together, there's a hidden world of effort, anxiety, and a lot of hard work powering their progress. Appreciate the effort beneath the calm exterior.

KENNISM: "They didn't see the late nights, the sacrifices, the quiet hustle behind the calm. They clapped at the promotion, but not the preparation. I don't share this for applause—I share it so someone else knows the stillness up top doesn't mean it's easy underneath. Like the duck, I stayed in motion beneath the surface—not for attention, but for alignment with my purpose. And by grace, I kept gliding." And if you ever feel like you're barely keeping your head above water, appreciate the fact that you're not alone. We're all ducks out here, doing our best to look cool while secretly paddling for our lives.

Chapter 4

I Can See Now

One thing I do know. I was blind but now I see.

—John 9:25

Clarity

"As I look back, I realize that only in hindsight could I finally see the lessons life was teaching me."

THE DOUBLE-EDGED SWORD OF CLARITY

Sometimes, if a person can't see what you see, they can't go where you are going! But, if you can see what others do not see, you can have what others do not have! And if by chance they do see something in you that you don't, there can be value in their perspective; sometimes you have to believe in someone's belief in you until you have belief in yourself.

But, even if they don't, it's **OK**. So often, we lose confidence in ourselves because of a past failure. The problem is that we will not forgive ourselves and try to move on. We will just live in it! We take that moment and let it direct the rest of our lives. It's **OK** to have doubt, but you cannot live in it. Remember, it is **OK** when others cannot see or understand your journey!

THE LONELINESS OF VISION

Can I just tell you, sometimes your own clarity can be lonely? When you finally see the path ahead, when the fog lifts and the horizon stretches out before you, it tends to make you super happy. But it can also feel isolating. Sometimes, no matter how brightly the future gleams in your eyes, no one else can see it.

Trust me, I learned this the hard way. First, it was with small things—ideas I had, dreams I shared. I'd sit across from friends bursting with excitement as I described what I could see so clearly in my mind: a new career path, a creative project, a move to a new city. "Can't you see it?" I'd ask, my hands gesturing wildly as if I could paint the picture for them with my words alone. I tend to talk with my hands, anyway, so I knew they would get the picture. But their faces would stay blank, their smiles polite but unconvincing.

"That sounds … interesting," they'd say, their tone seemed to doubt me.

And just like that, my excitement would deflate, like a balloon pricked by a needle of skepticism. That's why you can't tell everybody everything! Some things, ideas, projects, plans, were meant JUST FOR YOU and YOU ALONE! People will not see what you see because it isn't meant for them to see. And that's when it hit me: Not everyone is supposed to go where I'm going.

NOT EVERYONE'S SUPPOSED TO COME WITH YOU

Some people can't walk with you because their vision is tethered to where they are now. They're rooted in the familiar, in what's safe and predictable. It's not that they don't care about you; it's just that their eyes aren't built to see beyond their current space. Do not let that bother you. It's OK. But I have to admit, for a long time, I would let their inability to see hold me back. Their doubts became my doubts. Their fears became my fears. What if they were right? What if this dream of mine was too big, too risky? What if I were wrong?

I almost gave up on my vision because it was too bright for them. I say almost, because that's when I put the sunglasses on. I would think, why couldn't they just believe in me? Why couldn't they trust that I knew what I was doing? And there it was: Because this isn't their journey—it's mine.

THE SUNGLASSES MOMENT

My vision wasn't meant to be validated by others; remember I said earlier, my mom always told me I was special and "unikue," and I was finally beginning to own it. It wasn't someone else's job to understand—it was mine to follow through. Because of my mom's encouragement, I stopped looking for approval from people who couldn't see what I saw. Instead, I learned to trust myself—to trust the clarity of my own vision and started to live in my own purpose.

Clarity is a bit like putting on prescription glasses for the first time—you don't even realize how blurry things were until suddenly, it's all sharp. And once you've seen clearly, it's hard to go back to squinting just to make others comfortable.

VISION DOESN'T WAIT FOR VALIDATION

Now, don't get it twisted, I am human, and there are days when doubt creeps back in, whispering that maybe they were right after all. But every time that happens, I remind myself: They can't go where you're going because they weren't meant to.

Step by step, even as I am writing these words, I continue to walk my own path—even when it feels like no one else understands where I am headed or why I am going there in the first place. The most amazing thing happens when you buy into your purpose. Once you start moving forward with conviction, something magical happens: The right people begin to show up along the way—people who can see what you see or who trust you enough to follow and also lead if that is their purpose in your life for that time, even if they don't fully understand yet.

KENNISM: You can have physical vision, but still be spiritually blind, "your eyes are wide shut"—to believe the impossible, you can see the invisible! Even if no one else ever joins me on this journey, in search of my NEXT, I know one thing for certain: This road IS MINE to walk. And now? Now I can see so clearly that it doesn't matter who can or cannot see alongside me anymore. Because sometimes clarity isn't about convincing others—it's about having the courage to keep going even when no one else understands. Real vision has more to do with my insight than my eyesight.

Chapter 5

Is the Juice Worth the Squeeze

A heart at peace gives life to the body, but envy rots the bones.

— Proverbs 14:30

Peace

"It only matters if it brings you peace!"

There will be times in life when others ruffle your feathers or betray your trust—coworkers, friends, even family. The easy way out is to lash out, complain, or get even. After all, we feel justified. We were wronged! But before you speak or act, ask yourself, "Is it worth it?"

Psychologists have found that holding on to anger or bitterness doesn't just cloud our spirit—it actually harms the body. Research from Johns Hopkins Medicine shows that forgiveness can lower stress, reduce blood pressure, and even strengthen the immune system. It turns out that peace literally gives life to the body, just as the proverb says.

When your heart is hurt and your words want to fire off, pause. Because what we speak flows directly from what's in our hearts. Angry words may feel good in the moment, but they often leave lasting damage—to relationships, and to our own sense of peace.

THE BITTERNESS TRAP: BEFORE YOU LASH OUT ... ASK WHY?

The Bible says, "For the mouth speaks what the heart is full of." Meaning, when your heart is hurt and angry, your words can make matters worse. Your words make you temporarily feel better, but may do lasting damage. They may portray you as a bitter person. Angry words don't help matters. With your words, you can build up or tear down.

Lots of times, you want to say something to that person. You're going to get them told. In other words, you are going to tell them off. Meanwhile, they aren't even thinking about you. You are the one with the worry. You are the mad one. Stop being bitter, because it isn't worth it. Why shorten your life worrying or being bitter? You cannot move forward in life being bitter. You are going through it because you are getting ready to GROW and be BLESSED! Let them do what they do, for let's not forget, that's who they are!

WHEN PEACE IS LOUDER THAN PETTY

I had to learn this the hard way.

During my tenure as Assistant Dean at a specialized federal training university, I found myself cast as an outcast—not for lack of skill or vision, but because I didn't fit the culture. My professionalism—the suits, the polish, the standards— made others uncomfortable. My supervisor smiled to my face but whispered behind my back that my "leadership style" wasn't right for the team.

And let me tell you, it wasn't just subtle glances or side-eyes. My senior leader would smile and say, "Oh, Kenneth, you're doing an amazing job!" then turn around and tell my colleagues, "He's too much; I don't agree with his leadership style." I wasn't surprised at all, for she was known for saying, "I prefer to be liked than respected."

Whew. That one almost made me drop the mic. I mean, I wanted to go in. Give her a piece of my very composed but very sharp mind. But something in me—maybe my upbringing, maybe my faith, maybe my mother's voice— said, "Hold your mule." (Her way of saying hold your peace before you lose your power.)

I had to ask myself: Was the juice worth the squeeze? Was proving a point worth compromising my peace? That moment didn't break me. It refined me. Because the truth is, if everyone can handle your shine, then your light may not be bright enough.

I know what you are thinking. They always have something to say. That is a part of life. People always have something to say, always attacking, always criticizing. You heard it before: The enemy only attacks that which is of value to the person. Sometimes we cause self-inflicted wounds. Don't let the enemy in. Most of the time, it's all in the way you perceive it or how they perceive you. We all have to live with perception.

Leadership expert Daniel Goleman calls this emotional self-regulation—the ability to pause before reacting. Studies show that emotionally intelligent leaders are more respected and trusted in the long run because they choose peace over pride. That moment didn't break me. It refined me.

PERCEPTION AIN'T ALWAYS REALITY—BUT IT'S STILL A BATTLE

How others perceive you is their reality. They analyze you, dissect you. If you're skinny, you're starving yourself. If you're fat, you need to lose weight. If you leave your hair gray, you're getting old. If you color your hair, you're trying to act young. If you're dressed well, you're conceited. If you're dressed down, you've let yourself go. If you speak your mind, you're rude. If you don't say anything, you have no backbone. If you cry, you are weak. If you're sociable, you run the streets too much. If you stay to yourself, you're an introvert (standoffish, stuck up, etc.). If you have a nice life, you're a snob. And if you're educated and successful, you're bougie. YOU can't do anything without being criticized.

People will always have opinions. Social psychologists call this the halo effect: the human tendency to let one visible trait shape an entire impression. If you speak boldly, you're "arrogant." If you stay quiet, you "lack confidence." The danger isn't what they say—it's when we start believing them.

However, the challenge is not to let their perception become your prison. We live in a society where people can't seem to survive if they're not judging the next person. Leave them alone. Remember, vengeance is not yours; they will get what they deserve, without you helping that situation out. Greater HE that is in YOU than he that is in the world!

LET THE PEACE SPEAK LOUDER THAN THE PAIN

As I reflected on the journey that has brought me to this moment, I realized that the question of whether the juice was worth the squeeze was not about the external outcomes or the opinions of others. It was about the peace that came from within. The peace that came from knowing that I had given my all, that I had pursued my passions with integrity, and that I had learned to cherish every moment—both the triumphs and the setbacks.

As I looked out at the world around me, I saw that everyone was on their own journey, each with their own version of the squeeze. Some were struggling, others were thriving, but all were searching for that elusive sense of peace. And in that moment, I understood that the true value of any pursuit lies not in its external validation, but in the peace it brings to our hearts; yes, that inner peace that even the world can't take away.

In the end, peace isn't the absence of noise—it's the calm that remains despite it. Neuroscientists now know that reflection, prayer, and gratitude actually rewire the brain to respond with calm instead of chaos. That's the peace that "surpasses all understanding."

The journey may be long, winding, and sometimes arduous, but if it leads us to a place of peace, then yes, the juice is most certainly worth the squeeze. For in the end, it is not the destination that defines us, but the peace we find along the way. And it is this peace that makes every moment, every struggle, and every triumph worthwhile.

KENNISM: Love me or hate me, I am who I am, and there is no bigger judge than God! Believe that! Get to know people before judging them. Because, whether you like it or not, unless they wear a diaper, you can't change them. Be patient with your process—you won't regret what you don't say nearly as much as what you do. Hold your peace. That's where your power lives!

Chapter 6

The Onion Effect—Every Layer Tells a Story

Those who sow with tears will reap with songs of joy.

— Psalms 126:5

Emotional Strength, not Weakness

"Crying isn't weakness; it's a healthy release."

"TOO SENSITIVE"? THANK YOU. IT'S CALLED DEPTH

They used to call me "too sensitive." I've been told I feel too deeply, care too hard, and show too much. But here's the truth: Maybe they were not sensitive enough; feeling is not a flaw—it's a form of intelligence. That's what I call the "onion effect": when you start peeling back the layers of your soul—you know, anger, frustration, even silence, and find that underneath is pain, passion, purpose … and sometimes, tears.

The onion effect is what happens when we strip away our protective layers and let our true feelings show, resulting in those tears. Just like peeling an onion can sting, digging into our own feelings can be uncomfortable, but it's a sign of growth and healing. Crying isn't weakness—it's a natural response to facing what's real beneath the surface.

TEARS DON'T WEAKEN–THEY WATER

Every tear is proof that you're brave enough to feel, to heal, and to be authentically you. The tears are nothing more than emotional honesty. Tears are not signs of weakness— they are cherished expressions of pain, healing, and courage. I've shed silent tears at my desk. Tears in hallways. Not because I couldn't lead, but because leading meant carrying things others never saw.

And let's be real—some of us are walking around like emotional Vidalia onions. Sweet on the outside, but one honest conversation away from turning into a puddle. That's not a flaw—it's flavor! People who've been through some things tend to have the richest layers. I was always told that I was too sensitive. There was a time when that would bother me, but now if someone says, "You're too sensitive," I simply smile and nod and say, "Thank you. It's called depth."

Sensitivity is not a defect—it's a detector. It picks up on what's unsaid, it reads the room, it sees pain behind the performance. Reclaiming sensitivity is reclaiming power. In a world that profits from performance, your tears are a protest. In a society that praises composure, your emotion is courage. And if they say you're too emotional—thank them —it's confirmation you're still human.

Besides, bottled-up emotions are like forgotten onions in the back of the pantry—eventually, they'll start to stink. Better to let it out before things get funky. Laughter and tears are both ways your body hits the emotional reset button. So yes, cry if you need to. Laugh afterward if you can. And if you're lucky, do both at once—it burns calories and confuses people. And there's nothing like getting your endorphins working.

Peeling back your emotional layers doesn't make you fragile —it makes you fierce. It takes strength to sit with your feelings instead of running from them. Real courage is crying and still showing up the next day. It's being honest with yourself even when it's hard. Anyone can wear a mask; it takes guts to take it off and say, "This is me, flaws and all." Strength isn't about having a stone face—it's about having a soft heart that still beats strong after everything it's been through.

VULNERABILITY ISN'T WEAKNESS— IT'S YOUR SOUL LIFTING WEIGHTS

Let's stop glorifying emotional numbness as toughness. Strength isn't the absence of emotion; it's the ability to carry it with grace. The strongest people aren't those who never bend—they're the ones who bend, stretch, maybe even break for a moment, but they get back up. You know what takes more muscle than holding it in? Letting it out and trusting that you'll survive the storm inside.

So next time life hands you an onion moment, don't hold back. Let the tears fall and the healing begin. Because the truth is, you're not falling apart—you're peeling back to the best version of yourself.

KENNISM: Every tear you've cried, every layer you've peeled back, every moment you've faced yourself in the mirror and still chosen to love the reflection staring back—that's power. That's the kind of strength the world needs; not brute force, but brave hearts; not stone walls, but solid foundations. When you own your truth, when you embrace your scars and call them stories, you become unshakable. And that's something no one can take from you. Don't confuse my tears with weakness. My tears are fertilizer. They grow things: grace, grit, and greatness.

Chapter 7

Success Teaches You Nothing

Not only so, but we also glory in our sufferings, because we know that suffering produces perseverance; perseverance, character; and character, hope.

— Romans 5:3–4

Humility

"I've learned more from the moments that broke me than the ones that celebrated me. Failure's been a better teacher than applause ever was."

Your success is built on failure.

You don't have all you want, but you have more than you deserve.

Stop talking about what you lack and build on what you have.

"Favor" is what promotes you, not people.

You can't always look like where you've been, you've got to look like where you are going!

SUCCESS CELEBRATES, BUT FAILURE EDUCATES

Success is commanding. It feels like the ultimate reward for your hard work, determination, and talent. When you achieve it, the world celebrates, and you relish in the glow of your accomplishment. But here's the uncomfortable truth: It is my belief that success teaches you nothing!

Go ahead and say it; that sounds counterintuitive, even harsh. After all, isn't success what we're all striving for? Society has led us to believe we have done something right, correct? Yes, but success is seductive—it lulls you into a false sense of security. It makes you believe that you have arrived, you have figured it out, and, quite frankly, there is nothing else to learn. It's that part where the danger comes from. It's just an illusion, you see; when we succeed, we rarely stop to question what could have gone wrong or what we might have overlooked.

Success tends to blind us to our weaknesses because it doesn't demand introspection. It doesn't force us to confront our mistakes or challenge our assumptions. Instead, it reinforces the status quo. But here's the thing: Success is often built on a foundation of failure. Every achievement is preceded by countless missteps, wrong turns, and lessons learned the hard way. It's in those moments of failure—not success—that growth truly happens.

THE HUMBLE TEACHER NAMED FAILURE

Let's talk about that growth; it surely comes from failure. You may ask why. OK, glad you asked. Failure forces us to confront reality and ask tough questions: Why didn't this work? What did I miss? How can I do better next time? It's at that moment you become humble—yes, humility is powerful. It puts you in the decisive moment. Failure demands humility and resilience. It forces you to want to improve, adapt, innovate, and most importantly, develop!

One of the humblest men, in my opinion, was one of history's greatest innovators: Thomas Edison. It was noted that while trying to invent the lightbulb, he had failed in 10,000 attempts. Someone would ask how it felt to know he had failed in 10,000 tries. His response was golden, "I have not failed. I've just found 10,000 ways that wouldn't work." Each failure taught him something new and brought him closer to success. Without those failures, there would have been no light bulb!

SUCCESS IS A SNAPSHOT–NOT THE WHOLE STORY

This is why I continued to "hustle"; because I knew there was always something better, or a better way to do something or say something, all the while keeping me from becoming complacent. For me, it's like being nervous before doing a big speech that you have practiced and rehearsed or before taking an exam that you studied for all week and know all the answers—nervousness "keeps you humble."

Success is the same. You start to believe that success is inevitable or that your current approach will always work. Life has a way of humbling us when we least expect it. Failure is the experience! Failure is the feedback! Failure is a lesson!

THE BAMBOO LESSON

The story of the Chinese bamboo tree reminds us that real growth begins in silence. For years, after being planted, the seed shows no visible sign of life—no sprout, no leaf, no progress above ground. But beneath the surface, it's grinding. It's building roots deep enough, wide enough, strong enough to carry the weight of what's coming.

Then, almost suddenly, in just a few weeks, it shoots upward, rising over 80 feet. But here's the truth: It didn't grow in six weeks. It grew in the five silent years before that. In the dark. In obscurity.

See, it's not success that shaped the bamboo—it was the struggle, the waiting, the quiet preparation. Success didn't teach it anything; it only revealed what was already built.

Likewise, your success won't define you—your hard work will. Because success rarely teaches. It just tells the story of what you've already learned.

KENNISM: Success may be the destination, but failure is the journey—and it's on that journey where we discover who we really are. The next time you stumble or think you are falling short of your goals, IT'S OK! Remember that every successful person has walked this path before you—and that each failure brings you one step closer to greatness.

Because, at the end of the day, success teaches you nothing —but failure teaches you everything. Thanks to my colleague, manager, and friend, "AC," who inspired me to write this chapter. Success doesn't shape you—it exposes you. You grow in the dark, not in the spotlight.

Chapter 8

'Cause You Let Me

You have made your back like the ground—like a street for people to walk on.

— Isaiah 51:23

Responsibility

"You set the standard for how others interact with you. By accepting poor treatment without pushback, you indirectly endorse it."

WELL ... YOU LET ME!

Maybe you missed a flight, missed a meal, or missed some excellent opportunity to do something only because you were trying to look out for someone else. In your mind, you were being the big person, the nice guy, the nice girl! It ain't funny, but the joke is on you! You thought you were doing the person a favor, but the fact of the matter is, you were bothered by it because you gave in. On top of all of this, the person appears to have not appreciated what you've done. Heck, they didn't even say "thank you," and it appears they are taking advantage of you. But hold up— look a little deeper.

That person standing in front of you, reading your eyes, clocking your body language. They're not just disrespecting your boundaries. They're silently saying, "Well, you let me." Did you do it expecting a thank you in return? If you did, then you were doing it for the wrong reason! You should never put yourself in a position that you cannot control!

THE TRUTH HURTS ... BUT IT ALSO HEALS

There's a hard truth we often avoid confronting: Nothing can happen to you unless it happens through you. No one can walk over you unless you lie down first. It's easy to point fingers, to blame someone else for taking advantage of us, using us, or treating us poorly. The reality is, people can only do to you what we allow. If you let it happen, you can't complain about it, because there is also another truth to this: You hold the power to change it.

Allow me to let you in on a little secret. When someone mistreats you, your first instinct might be to say, "They should know better!" But here's the kicker—they often don't. Why? Because you trained them. Yep, you taught them with your silence, our second changes, your "it's fine" shrugs. To them, it wasn't mistreatment—it was permission. And in their head, they're not apologizing, they're thinking, "Well, you let me!" Here's the thing: every time they crossed a line, there was a moment where you could have said, "No." A moment where you could have spoken up, set a boundary, or walked away. Instead, for whatever reason—you don't like conflict, you have a love for them, or maybe you just doubt yourself, but either way—you stayed silent. Silence, my friend, in today's society, is often interpreted as approval.

Seemingly, everyone wants something for nothing. Really, they are taking what you give them. If you offer your time without limits, they'll take it. If you give your energy without requiring reciprocity, they'll absorb it. If you let them disrespect you without consequence, they'll assume it's OK to keep doing it. And wait, this isn't about blaming yourself for someone else's bad behavior—it's about recognizing your role in allowing it to continue, 'cause you let me!

BUILD SPEED BUMPS, NOT WALLS

Something I had to learn over the years and continue to absorb in my daily life, especially when it comes to relationships—whether romantic, platonic, or professional—you have to set boundaries. Now I know what you are thinking. Sir, if I set a boundary, it may seem like a guard keeping people out. On the contrary, boundaries are like bridges if you build them correctly; they teach people how to treat you while still allowing them to stay connected to you, respecting you, your space, and your ground rules. OK, here is something else you can consider. If you are allowing someone to repeatedly run over you, it's not their fault. Huh? We will talk more about this in the next chapter, "Non-Negotiable-#TheCostofCompromise"

NO SPEED BUMPS? EXPECT A HIT-AND-RUN!

Let me make it plain. If you live in a community with a lot of kids, you will typically see speed bumps to slow drivers down and encourage them to proceed with caution in that area. Same with relationships, you have to have speed bumps in place—they force people to slow down and consider their actions before proceeding (running over you). Call it crazy, but without them, people will keep driving at full speed because they don't see any reason not to. The good thing about these speed bumps is that you can have as many as you desire: this is what I need, this is what I will not tolerate, this is what I like, this is what I do not like. It may take some time to adopt, but you will surely find out who respects you and who doesn't. Tough lesson I had to learn. It's all about accountability, and it starts with you! I know you have heard it before, "you've got to love yourself first"!

Bottom line, you may not be able to control how others treat you, but you sure can control how much access they have to your time and energy. And remember, it is OK to say NO! Respecting you and your space comes with a price. And if they don't respect those rules, then maybe it was meant to be a "temporary relationship."

There will always be people who try to take advantage of your meekness, treating it as weakness. But you get to decide how much access they have to your heart? You get to decide where the line is drawn.

KENNISM: I can't complain if I let it happen. Going forward, I have learned to forgive them for taking advantage of me, but more importantly, to forgive myself for allowing it to happen. My mom would always say, "If people knew better, they would do better." Well, now is my time to tell 'em! And I hope that, at the end of the day, the right people respect my territory and give back in equal measure. If I do this right, I hope the wrong people will fall away when I stop letting them take advantage of me.

Midbook Review

A QUICK PAUSE—AND A SMALL ASK

If you're here, you've already invested time, thought, and reflection into *Hustle While You Wait*.

That matters.

If something in these pages has resonated with you so far—challenged your thinking, affirmed your journey, or encouraged you during a season of waiting—I'd like to invite you to share that experience.

You don't have to finish the book to leave a review on **Amazon**.

A few honest words about how the book is impacting you right now can help another reader decide to begin—or keep going.

You don't need perfect language.

Just your perspective.

YOU MIGHT SHARE:

• What has stood out to you so far

• A chapter or idea that made you pause and reflect

• How the message connects to your current season

If you would like to stay connected with Kenneth LeGrand and explore additional insights, encouragement, and updates on his work, visit **kenlegrandauthor.com**. The site provides resources and guidance designed to help readers stay focused, faithful, and productive while navigating seasons of preparation and growth.

Thank you for continuing the journey through *Hustle While You Wait*.

Chapter 9

Non-Negotiable— #TheCostofCompromise

All you need to say is simply "Yes" or "No"; anything beyond this comes from the evil one.

— Matthew 5:37

In other words, integrity doesn't stutter—it stands.

Let's see how we can get beyond "'Cause You Let Me"!

Boundaries

"A boundary you negotiate away is no boundary at all."

There's a reason boundaries exist. Not to keep people out, but to keep you intact. Over nearly four decades of service, I learned this the hard way. Every time you compromise what you believe just to fit in, keep the peace, or earn approval, you chip away at who you are. Bit by bit. If you're not careful, one day you'll look in the mirror and won't recognize what's left.

In modern leadership psychology, boundaries are considered one of the clearest indicators of emotional intelligence. Brené Brown calls them "the distance at which I can love you and me simultaneously." In over thirty years of leadership, I learned that boundaries aren't barriers—they're the backbone of self-respect.

STANDING FIRM IN A SHIFTING WORLD

I was never interested in being one of the "cool kids." I didn't care to go along just to get along. Early on, I learned: If you don't define your boundaries, someone else will—and they won't do it with your best interests in mind. I didn't chase approval because I knew compromise might win me favor for a moment, but it would cost me eventually. That's a price too high for any title, promotion, or applause.

Saying "no" isn't resistance—it's self-respect. And standing firm doesn't make you rigid—it makes you reliable.

THE DISCIPLINE OF INTEGRITY

Harvard Business Review calls integrity "the invisible contract between trust and accountability." When that contract is broken, people don't just lose confidence in you —they lose safety in your leadership.

I've lived by this simple, powerful truth: "Let your yes be yes, and your no be no." Not from a place of pride, but from a place of purpose. Because the moment you start bending your values, you begin drifting away from who you truly are.

As Polonius wisely counseled in Shakespeare's *Hamlet*, "To thine own self be true." Shakespeare wasn't writing about management, but his wisdom still applies to every boardroom and briefing room.

That line has echoed through centuries because integrity doesn't expire—it evolves. Authenticity is not trendy—it's timeless.

WHEN BOUNDARIES BREAK, IDENTITY FADES

In today's culture of quick gains and brand over character, it's easy to forget that the strongest brands are built on unshakable beliefs.

When you negotiate your boundaries—whether it's for acceptance, convenience, or short-term success—you begin to chip away at your foundation. Piece by piece, your moral compass dulls. Your no becomes soft. Your identity becomes a performance, not a conviction. Eventually, you'll find yourself living for the applause, not for the purpose.

I've seen this happen too many times. Gifted professionals lose their way—not because they lack skill, but because they forgot who they were. The truth: When you abandon your values to climb the ladder, the climb may be swift, but the fall is even faster. You can't sustain greatness on a fractured foundation.

BOUNDARIES BUILD LEGACY

I offer this challenge to leaders, professionals, and anyone navigating difficult spaces: Hold your boundaries like your breath depends on it—because in many ways, it does.

Boundaries are the guardrails of integrity. They are not just lines we draw in the sand; they are the evidence of our self-respect, the non-negotiables of our identity. Boundaries are what allow you to lead without losing yourself. They make sure your influence remains clean, your name stays credible, and your peace remains intact.

ANCHORED, NOT MOVED

True influence isn't loud—it's anchored. It's the calm you carry when chaos circles you. Leaders are always watched —not when they speak, but when they stand.

People notice when you refuse to bend where others break. They draw strength from your steadiness and courage from your consistency. Your boundaries don't just protect you; they give others permission to protect themselves, too.

KENNISM: I have lived this message. I have fought for this boundary. And I stand—not because I was never tested, but because I refused to be reshaped by the pressures around me. Stay true. Stay grounded. Stay unmoved. Your presence loses power when it comes at the expense of your principles. The moment may pass, but the movement? Legacy.

Chapter 10

It Was Meant to Be Temporary

There is a time for everything, and a season for every activity under the heavens.

— Ecclesiastes 3:1

Acceptance

"I finally understood that some things are meant to be temporary—and that's OK."

TRYING TO HOLD ON TO WHAT'S ALREADY LET GO

Stop investing in folks who are not feeling you. How often do we try to hold onto relationships, friendships, or jobs, only to find out it was meant to be temporary? Yes temporary! Sometimes the wrong doors must close so the right ones can open. Same with your so-called friends;

sometimes the wrong ones have to leave to make room for the right ones.

Instead, we try to make people significant when they are not! You did not know it, but they did. You just couldn't bring yourself to accept it. With your sensitive, over-caring heart, you sit there asking yourself, "What did I do to deserve this?"

I asked myself: What did I say? What did I do? And more painfully, what could I have done differently?

You're scratching your head, replaying conversations in your mind like a broken record. You try to reach out, hoping for a response, but there's nothing. Just silence. And that silence is louder than any words they could've said.

THEY LEFT BECAUSE YOU WERE BEING YOU

From experience, I will share with you these two things: 1) If your absence doesn't affect them, then your presence never mattered, and 2) It is nothing you did wrong and nothing you said. In fact, being you is what caused it. You were just being your authentic self; you shared information, you shared laughs, you listened, and you were there when they needed you. You contributed to their growth, and now that they are all grown up, your services are no longer needed.

I know that sounds harsh, and I must admit, at first, it can be very disheartening. But the more I thought about it, it's really complimentary. In general, some people are seasonal. Yes seasonal! Should I explain? OK, I will.

After all, life is about giving! Is that not what the Good Book says—***In everything I did, I showed you that by this kind of hard work we must help the weak, remembering the words the Lord Jesus himself said: It is more blessed to give than to receive*** (Acts 20:35). ***We then that are strong ought to bear the infirmities of the weak, and not to please ourselves*** (Romans 15:1). I know what you are thinking. This is a tough pill to swallow. Get over it, let it go, let it die, bury it, and don't dig it up!

If you continue to harbor it, you put yourself in a vulnerable and wounded position. My experience has taught me that wounded people wound people, broken people break people, and healed people heal people. Sure, those people came into your life, and it was temporary. It's time to release them, no hard feelings. If you are unforgiving, it impedes healing and your growth. As you forgive them, you also need to forgive yourself. What you do not want is for anything or anyone to hamper you from reaching your destiny. Continue to align yourself with those who believe in you and your destiny. Trust me. Now that you have gone through this moment, you will immediately know who is for you, going forward. You have the experience!

YOU CAN'T MOVE FORWARD LOOKING BACKWARD

What does move forward mean? OK, you have to stop looking for your future with the images of your past! You cannot move forward in life being bitter! What is done, is done! Do not resurrect what has been buried: your past. As well, do not punish what is alive: your future, your new beginning, your destiny. As I look back, staring at the remnants of what once was, my heart sometimes gets heavy, but my mind is finally clear. For so long, I had held on—clutching memories, dreams, and pieces of a life that no longer fit me. I would often tell myself it was worth saving, worth fighting for, but deep down, I knew the truth: It was meant to be temporary.

Even now, if I am honest, the words echo in my head like a quiet plea: Leave it behind. Drop it and move on. At first, they felt harsh, almost cruel. But now I understand. They weren't words of defeat; they were words of freedom. Not everything is meant to last forever, and that doesn't make it any less meaningful. It just means its time has passed. I take a deep breath, feeling the weight I'd been carrying for far too long begin to lift. It wasn't easy to let go—it never is—but holding on had been slowly breaking me. And I realized that by clinging to what was gone, I was losing sight of everything still waiting for me.

IT'S NOT CLOSURE—IT'S PEACE

I made a choice. In a quiet moment, with no audience and no applause, I released it—not with bitterness or anger, but with gratitude. Gratitude for the lessons it taught me, for the strength it revealed in me, and for the quiet nudge to keep moving forward. As I turned from the past, I felt something shift—not closure exactly (because let's be honest, we rarely get that), but something close. Acceptance. And with that acceptance came peace.

I remind myself often, "It's OK to let go." And each time I do, a small, knowing smile creeps across my face—because I know I've finally embraced the freedom of moving forward.

KENNISM: Don't cheat your future by worrying about your past, because it's over. Everything in your life is a reflection of a choice you made. If you want different results, you have to make different choices. In the big scheme of things, it's small compared to where your future lies. It's like the rearview mirror on a vehicle—it is smaller than your windshield, but do you know why? Glad you asked. I heard Pastor Tony Evans put it this way. He said it is "because where you are going is BIGGER than where you have been." You cannot fix yesterday, but you can begin preparing for your tomorrow. Finally, just because it was good doesn't mean it was meant to last. Some assignments are seasonal—and knowing when to move is just as important as knowing when to stay.

Chapter 11

Do What Is Sustainable

Let us not become weary in doing good, for at the proper time we will reap a harvest if we do not give up.

— Galatians 6:9

There was a point in my career when I thought running faster meant leading better. I was juggling projects, mentoring people, and chasing outcomes—until my body and spirit reminded me that fatigue isn't a badge of honor. That's when I learned that leadership without sustainability is just motion without meaning.

Sustainability

"I am not about the moment, but about the movement."

Doing what's sustainable means resisting the temptation to chase short-term applause while ignoring long-term impact.

It's about legacy—planting seeds that may not bear fruit until years later. When I invested time in mentoring young professionals or modernizing systems no one thought would change, I wasn't working for immediate results. I was building a foundation that others could stand on long after I left the room.

Psychologists like Walter Mischel, known for the famous "marshmallow experiment," showed that people who practice delayed gratification often experience greater long-term success. The same principle applies to leadership: True progress rewards patience.

Remember: *What you do today is NOT for today. It's for tomorrow.* The small, consistent moves—the sacrifices nobody sees— are shaping your future more than any headline moment ever will.

LEGACY IS BUILT IN THE QUIET

Success comes in many forms. For some, advancing in their professional life, climbing the corporate ladder, or building a business from the ground up exemplifies success. For others, it's maintaining a healthy lifestyle, reaching a weight goal, or finally feeling comfortable in their own skin. Sometimes, success is simply having peace of mind— knowing that you're making the best choices for your future self.

Whatever your version of success may be, one truth remains: It must be sustainable to be meaningful. A Harvard Business Review study found that leaders who intentionally build renewal habits—time for reflection, rest, and faith—report higher engagement and longevity. Sustainability isn't about doing the most today; it's about making intentional choices that prepare you for success tomorrow.

SUSTAINABILITY IS A DISCIPLINE, NOT A BUZZWORD

It's about making tough calls today to protect your tomorrow:

- Saying no to opportunities that look good but don't align with your purpose.
- Choosing rest when your body demands it, even when the hustle culture says "keep pushing."
- Investing in relationships and mentorships that outlast titles and paychecks.
- Preparing the next generation through coaching and mentoring so the mission outlives the position.
- Recognizing that longevity isn't luck—it's built on daily choices. Every yes and no compound over time.

Nobel laureate Daniel Kahneman wrote about our tendency toward "fast thinking"—reacting for speed instead of reflection. Sustainability is the counterbalance; it asks us to slow down enough to ensure our actions match our intentions.

BEWARE THE ILLUSION OF FAST RESULTS

We live in a culture of quick fixes and instant gratification. "Lose 20 pounds and get six-pack abs in 10 days!" I've tried that, with no success. Real transformation takes more than a meal plan or a week of planks. The slow discipline builds not just muscle but mindset. Quick results fade. Consistency sticks.

Chasing shortcuts might feel exciting, but real growth—sustainable growth—takes time, discipline, and patience. Shortcuts rarely last. Faster isn't always better; coordinated hustle is. Sustainability is not about slowing ambition—it's about aligning energy with purpose.

SUSTAINABILITY MEANS ALIGNMENT

Sustainability doesn't mean staying comfortable or avoiding change. It means pacing yourself so you don't burn out before reaching your destination. It's having the courage to grow gradually and the wisdom to know that slow progress is still progress.

Burnout researcher Christina Maslach and Michael Leiter found that fatigue often stems from misalignment—when what we do contradicts what we value. Sustainability isn't softness; it's alignment. When your goals, energy, and faith work together, you build not just success, but peace.

In my own thirty-nine years of federal service, I've seen many sprint through marathons—brilliant minds who moved fast but lacked endurance. Doing what's sustainable means creating systems, habits, and boundaries that protect your peace, health, and legacy.

PEACE IS THE PROOF

When you do what is sustainable:

- You prioritize rest as much as progress—six to seven hours of sleep at a minimum!
- You build for the long term—the movement, not just the moment.
- You pursue goals that match your capacity, not someone else's highlight reel.
- You embrace authenticity—sometimes you'll walk alone, and that's OK.

So today, whether you're questioning your career path, evaluating your health, or feeling overwhelmed by life's pace—pause, reflect, and ask yourself: Is this sustainable? If the answer is no, give yourself permission to change course. Sustainability isn't weakness—it's wisdom, maturity, and strength rooted in purpose.

KENNISM: "Success that breaks you is not success. But success that builds you—mind, body, and spirit—that's what lasts." When we chase success without intention, we build shaky foundations. We succeed on the outside but fall apart within. **True success isn't about speed; it's about stability and longevity.** Pace yourself—growth that lasts doesn't happen overnight. The goal isn't just to arrive; it's to **still be standing when you get there**. Hustling without intention leads to exhaustion, but hustling with **purpose** leads to fulfillment and peace.

Chapter 12

The Watchers—Here's What They Said ... What I Carry with Me Still

Let someone else praise you, and not your own mouth; an outsider, and not your own lips.

— Proverbs 27:2

Affirmation

"Sometimes it takes the words of others to remind me of my own strength."

My mother used to remind me, "You never know who's watching." At the time, I thought she meant be careful—but as I grew in leadership, I realized she meant be consistent. Every decision, every late night, every quiet act of integrity is seen by someone, even when you don't notice. Those words echo in this chapter, because what follows isn't about recognition—it's about reflection. Leadership leaves fingerprints, and these are the marks of that journey.

In the midst of life's journey, it's often the words of others that remind me of my strength—and the impact I've had, even when I didn't realize it. What follows is a collection of heartfelt sentiments, poems, and kind words that reflect the best in me, seen through the eyes of those I've walked beside. These testimonials don't just uplift—they ground me. They remind me that I've made a difference. And sometimes, that's exactly what we need: a mirror held up by love to remind us of who we are. I carry their words not as praise, but as fuel—to keep walking, keep leading, keep becoming, and most importantly, keep Hustling.

REFLECTIONS FROM EARLY DAYS

WHY ME?
By Valdenia Reaves McMillian, circa October 1998, to
Kenneth LeGrand

At times in life
When things get hard
I often look to Heaven
And ask the Lord—why me?

I try my best to communicate
With my people who are filled with hate
I open my arms for which to embrace
In turn, they spit right in my face
Why me?

From day to day, I open my heart
Someone drops in just to tear it apart
As I try to hide from these worldly fears
I find myself shedding numerous tears
Why me?

I show my face with a smile that shines
Another face frowns at mine
Yet I still try to help another
Who refuses to even call me brother
Why me?

It's me because ...
God chose a man
Who could take a stand
One who could lift his name in praise
And pray to him for better days

One who opens doors for others
And brings about peace to troubled brothers
One who is gentle and caring
And is known very well for giving and sharing

One who is very humble and wise
And is a Godly example in others' eyes
One who is not temperate or vain
And always uplifts Jesus's name.

Over the years, people have described me in many ways. I didn't ask for the titles—I just showed up, did the work, and tried to be who I said I was. But their words?

THE ROLES THEY SAW

- **Motivator:** A positive motivational influence
- **Teacher:** One who teaches others
- **Friend:** A person known well to another and regarded with liking, affections, and loyalty
- **Counselor:** A person who gives counsel
- **Leader:** One who leads or guides others
- **Helper:** A person who contributes to the fulfillment of a need
- **Mentor:** A wise and trusted counselor

THE BIRTH OF M2M–MENTOR TO MENTOR

I started a mentoring group—just six people at first. Nothing fancy. Just a space to talk, grow, and learn from each other. I called it M2M—Mentor to Mentor because that's exactly what it was. We weren't doing top-down lectures—we were sharing, building each other up. Over time, it grew. We ended up with over a hundred folks. It turned into something special—folks talking careers, getting guidance, hearing from senior leaders—the first of its kind.

One of the members gave me a dedication plaque one day. A simple gesture that meant the world. It said:

Mentor 2 Mentor

YOU Love the LORD and YOU are a Man of Character # YOU can't be Bought and YOUR Word is Bond # YOU Possess Opinions and YOU share them with Confidence and Dignity # YOU don't Hesitate to take Risks # YOU are Honest and YOU don't Compromise with Wrong # YOU are True to YOUR Friends through Good and Bad—in Adversity as well as Prosperity # YOU don't Beat Down You Build Up # YOU Care: YOU Give YOUR Best #

THROUGH THEIR EYES

During one of our mentoring sessions, I asked my colleagues a simple but powerful question: "When you hear my name, what comes to mind?" It's an exercise you might try yourself—a way to check how you're being received, to measure authenticity, or just to spark some self-reflection and growth.

To respect privacy, I've omitted full names and used initials instead—with their permission, of course. What follows is a collection of honest reflections.

THEMES OF LEGACY

DM: For me, I think of a man who's willing to put his own skin in the game to help others around him; probably in some cases, to his own detriment. And someone who clearly sees the challenges or problems that exist at this agency and is motivated to do something about them.

LM: Let's see ... first thoughts about Ken LeGrand: leader, integrity, cares about people, knowledgeable, honest, keeps it real.

JL: When I hear "Kenneth LeGrand," this is what I am hearing or envisioning:

- Warrior
- Passionate
- Bridge developer
- Lending a helping hand
- Unselfish
- Determined
- Outspoken
- Intentional
- Transparent Mentor
- Deliberate
- Respected
- Well-Known
- "The Sacrifice"

ET: Kenneth LeGrand is a man of spirituality; always willing to lend a helping hand and lots of wisdom. Kenneth is one who can be raw (no filter) but is also a man of self-reflection who seeks out ways to grow and improve. That being said, he is a person of self-awareness and easily identifies and vocalizes (which is rare) his weaknesses and strengths. He is a servant in many ways. I find it hard to believe that Kenneth ever meets a stranger; he is friendly, personable, and curious. He is always willing to help, willing to share his knowledge and his network; he is an advocate.

JD: "SHARP." You name it, and Kenneth LeGrand is SHARP!

- SHARP dresser

- SHARP intellect
- SHARP mind
- SHARP wit
- SHARP coach
- SHARP friend
- SHARP leader
- SHARP motivator
- SHARP constructive criticizer
- SHARP organizer
- SHARP ... everything! Never dull!

RS: When I hear the name Kenneth LeGrand, I think of a person whose leadership has inspired many, including me. A man who has been a wonderful mentor in the success of life and career journeys. Kenneth LeGrand is a name you hear, and everyone around has a great story to tell about his amazing work and all the effort he puts into it. I also think of M2M when I hear Kenneth LeGrand, because that's how I got accustomed to having wonderful mentors in my working environment. So, when you hear the name, you picture the face, the mindset, and the drive.

TK: I think you already know this, but my first thought is "fixer," a.k.a. Poppa Pope. You have a vast network and are always willing to reach out and help people. Not just in words, but you stick with it to completion ... until the person is in a new job or there's a peaceful resolution. You don't back down and are willing to die on a hill for others. At the same time, I can see where some of the battles have left you jaded with some of the processes here. You're a "feeler," so the battle makes you a bit weary at times.

ODL: When I hear your name mentioned, the first thing that comes to mind is that it is something good or something good is about to happen. Not having worked for or with you gives me that "outsider looking in" perspective. I see the passion that you have for M2M, and I am sure that carries into other aspects of your life. I see that you truly care about lifting others and want to see others doing the same. I see the spiritual side and how you are not ashamed of showing it. This is also something that I value and know has a great influence on the type of people that we are. These are just a few of the things that I have seen and are qualities of a great person.

TB: When I hear the name Kenneth LeGrand, three things initially come to mind: leadership, positivity, and encouragement.

Firstly, Ken's integrity and influence are essential leadership traits that he displays daily. For a leader to be successful, it is imperative that they have the qualities of integrity through transparency that Ken exhibits through various professional aspects; and his ability to convince people through logical, emotional, or cooperative appeals is also an important characteristic of his effective leadership. For example, he understands that everybody is different and is mindful of this fact when dealing with his co-workers and subordinates; this is a great skill he possesses.

Secondly, Ken has a positive outlook and is a positive thinker. He often thinks through how problems can be solved, while maintaining an air of amiability, so that he remains approachable, and his co-workers and subordinates are not fearful or weary of him. This trait is important because, if anyone under his leadership comes to him with a problem, having an approachable attitude like Ken's makes solving the problem much quicker and easier than it might otherwise be. Additionally, this quality of positivity makes his peers think positively, improving morale, which is especially important during these difficult times.

Thirdly, Ken has always provided encouragement and is continuously advocating for his co-workers and subordinates, and holds them fully accountable for their own actions. Ken consistently stands up for his teams, recognizes hard work when he sees it, and is not afraid to discipline those who do not behave appropriately under his guidance. Through his inspiration, he creates an environment of trust that improves effectiveness and cultivates a climate of excellence that is evident in his workplace.

In conclusion, Ken certainly has many more traits than the three mentioned above, but these come to mind first when I hear his name. Ken has a genuine concern for people and always helps others hone their own interpersonal skills and abilities through nurturing, development, and real-world experiences.

CG: When I hear the name Kenneth LeGrand, I automatically think: A great senior person who knows everything as it pertains to work, and if he doesn't, he definitely has the connections. I know there will be an answer to any question that I have. He is a person who always understands me and doesn't look down on others, always raising a person's hopes when in doubt. He is a strong advocate, a passionate leader, and the best senior leader the agency has to offer, but I fear there will never be another like him. So, with that being said, a one-and-only, strong leader, mentor, and friend. Thanks a lot, Kenny!

JM: This is awesome. Here's what I think of Ken:

- Someone who gives back and is willing to help in any way he can
- A true follower of Christ
- A very GENUINE person who cares
- A trusted mentor and friend
- Someone who keeps it 100%—no sugarcoating
- Someone who's a go-getter
- Someone who develops others
- An easy-going and funny person
- A leader
- Someone who goes against the grain—not ordinary

KR: Genuine comes to mind.

RR: I did work your assignment in my head—in fact it started that day, into the night, throughout the weekend (and also explained it to my hubby about feeling terrible 'bout it), and here we are today: kind, kind-hearted, caring sharing, fearless, professional, warrior, leader, strong yet sensitive, and man of valor, to name a few.

TE: A lot of people define success in different ways. I read in Earl Nightingale's book, *The Strangest Secret*, that he defined success as the progressive realization of a worthy ideal or goal. Another way that I've heard it defined, and one that I gravitate toward: Success is defined by how many people are better off because you lived. I can boldly and proudly say, I'm better off because of Kenneth LeGrand!

JK: When I hear your name, I think of a few things:

- Aggie through and through. Puts others before himself.
- Passed over for promotion for years, but doesn't let that stop him from sharing his knowledge with others.
- Believes in the concepts of advocacy and sponsorship.

KENNISM: Reading their words reminded me that the impact we leave isn't always loud—sometimes, it's quiet, personal, and deeply lasting. This wasn't about hearing my own praises, but about recognizing the power of showing up, staying consistent, and doing the work. These reflections aren't just a mirror—they're motivation. Not just for me, but for anyone committed to leading with integrity, even when no one's watching. What they saw in me helped me see myself more clearly. Their words weren't just compliments—they were confirmations. I carry them, not for validation, but as reminders of the value I bring and the lives I've touched. That's legacy.

Chapter 13

I Make No Apologies

For am I now seeking the approval of men, or of God? Or am I trying to please people? If I were still trying to please people, I would not be a servant of Christ.

— Galatians 1:10

Authenticity

"I make no apologies for being true to myself."

YOU WEREN'T IN THE ROOM

Oftentimes in life, you work hard to become all that you can be; no, not for the services, but from a personal standpoint. You work hard—making strides, doing the right thing, staying positive, helping others, and walking in favor. And just when you think the people closest to you would be happy for your progress, you're hit with a rude awakening. They begin to criticize you; make statements like, "you think you are all that," "you may have a degree, but that don't mean anything," just to name a couple. It gets so bad, you begin to feel guilty about all that you have done. You second-guess your career and your accomplishments. I say stop it! You have to get out of that funk. You have to wake up and realize that those folks were not there when you were up late studying and making the sacrifices to get to where you wanted to be. While you were "hustling while you waited," where were they?

That's why this chapter is called, "I Make No Apologies"! That's right, you owe no one any apologies for your hard work, your sacrifices, or your late nights. You did it! You and God! Count others' criticism as confirmation. It's your reminder that the light you carry makes some people squint. For this reason, I believe it is my responsibility to use my talents and gifts to bless others. I try to make it my mission to have folk leave me better than they came. If and when that happens, I feel I have done my job.

In leadership psychology, authenticity is not just confidence —it's alignment. Carl Rogers described it as "self-congruence," the harmony between who you are and how you show up. Adam Grant echoed this idea in his research on authentic leadership: People follow what's real, not what's rehearsed. The moment you edit yourself for approval, you begin losing the voice that made you worth following.

Leadership isn't easy. It carries its own weight—the sacrifice, the scrutiny, the sleepless nights. I've learned that every crown comes with a cost. Influence looks like privilege from a distance, but up close, it's a promise—a commitment to purpose, not comfort.

The real key is to stay ready. You were built with everything required for the journey—wisdom to discern, compassion to lead, and a value that doesn't depend on validation. The foundation is already in you. People will still talk, but perception is free—purpose is priceless.

PERCEPTION AIN'T TRUTH

Perception can become a prison. Others will dissect and define you, sometimes without ever knowing you. In my workplace, we used to call it the "hallway file"—a reputation built from whispers, not truth. You cannot let their perception become your prison. Their view of you isn't your reality. Keep pressing. They see your glory, but they don't know the work behind it.

Perception is who they say you are. Character is who you know you are. When perception becomes your prison, authenticity becomes your freedom. If people trust their opinion of you more than your reality, they were never meant to understand your journey.

To choose the uncommon path is to embrace the weight of a higher calling.

UNCOMMON ON PURPOSE

I refuse to live as the common man. To be uncommon is to invite criticism and to walk a road few understand. But it also means aligning with a higher calling—shaping your life with purpose under the guidance of your Creator.

In today's leadership climate, where personal brands rise faster than character is tested, authenticity still stands out. Harvard Business Review found that humility and integrity rank among the most powerful leadership traits tied to long-term influence—not charisma.

As Dean Alfange wrote in "My Creed" (printed in Reader's Digest in 1952):

It is my right to be uncommon—if I can.

I seek opportunity—not security. I do not wish to be a kept citizen, humbled and dulled by having the state look after me. I want to take the calculated risk; to dream and to build, to fail and to succeed. I refuse to barter incentive for a dole. I prefer the challenges of life to the guaranteed existence; the thrill of fulfillment to the stale calm of utopia. I will not trade freedom for beneficence nor my dignity for a handout. I will never cower before any earthly master nor bend to any threat.

It is my heritage to stand erect, proud, and unafraid; to think and act for myself, enjoy the benefit of my creations, and to face the world boldly and say, "This, with God's help, I have done."

The choice is yours. Being uncommon means standing for something when it would be easier to blend in. It means being authentic even when misunderstood, and walking in faith even when unseen. If you are crazy enough to believe you can—maybe you're exactly who God designed to prove that you can.

KENNISM: Make no apologies and be you. All others are taken. What others think of you is none of your business. Mom told me I was UNIKUE—and she was right. I wasn't built for approval; I was built for assignment. When you're built differently, folks won't always understand your blueprint. Let them whisper. Just make sure your walk keeps speaking louder.

Chapter 14

The Roots of My Rise

Start children off on the way they should go, and even when they are old, they will not turn from it.

— Proverbs 22:6

Foundation

"In this life, we accomplish nothing alone—my journey is no different."

No one becomes great alone. Not truly. Not ever!

I don't care what anyone says about being self-made—I know I had a village. A real one. Family, friends, and yes, even a few "frenemies" along the way. Each one taught me something.

For me, it all started with an intentional spirit, instilled in me and my siblings by our parents—the spirit of service.

Let me tell you a little more about that village and the ways they carried me into this transition.

My father, **Willie Sr.**, **the Foundation**, taught me it's not only acceptable—but powerful—to want your own things in your own time. Wanting more is not a weakness; it's wisdom. He'd smile and say, "Live happy—it beats being dead broke." And I believed him.

But more than that, my father was a man whose hands bore witness to work. He didn't just build things—he built belief. In us. In dreams. In doing things the right way, even when it wasn't the easy way. His lessons weren't lectures; they were lived. Quiet examples that spoke louder than words.

Those were the roots he gave us—silent, steady, strong—growing beneath the surface long before anyone saw the rise. Roots of resilience. Roots of faith. Roots that remind me that success without character is hollow, but character with endurance produces fruit that lasts.

When I stand firm today, when I hustle while I wait, when I choose movement over moments—it's because of the foundation he laid. My father didn't just raise a son, he planted a legacy.

My oldest brother, **Willie Jr.**, **the First Responder of Progress**, worked thirty-plus years with the State Department of Transportation as a Highway Emergency Response Operator—better known as a HERO. And that's exactly what he's been. Day after day, responding to traffic incidents, wrecks, flat tires, stranded families, and even broken limbs. His calling was simple on the surface—but powerful in practice: Keep things moving.

(Ever met an angry commuter stuck in traffic? Then you understand his ministry!) My brother's work wasn't just about clearing lanes; it was about clearing paths. About helping people get back on their journey when life threw them off course.

What I saw in him was more than a job—it was a living example. He taught me that no matter what others think, staying grounded is everything. Even when life pulls you in opposite directions, he would always remind me, "God has our back."

That calm under pressure became a spiritual seed for me. It taught me that purpose doesn't always come with applause, a spotlight, or a platform. Sometimes, purpose is simply being present in the storm—steady, faithful, and committed to service. And when you live like that, you don't just leave tire tracks on the highway, you leave footprints of faith on every life you touch.

My next oldest brother, **Ray**, **the Servant in Command**, served over twenty-five years in the US Air Force in Healthcare Administration, and every single year was anchored in purpose. He often describes it as "nothing more than being a servant to serve." But that simple phrase carries weight—because true leadership is rooted in service.

Even after hanging up the uniform, Ray never stopped serving. Through his work with the Men of Honor Foundation, he continues the mission of building young men—instilling values, teaching integrity, and shaping lives with purpose. His impact isn't just measured by the rank he wore or the titles he held, but by the character he helped form in others.

Ray showed me that moving forward doesn't mean abandoning your foundation. It means carving your own path while carrying the lessons of those before you. He has a way of saying it plain: "Live now—save dying for later." That's not just a phrase, it's a charge—to embrace the present, to pursue your calling with courage, and to pour into others while you still have breath.

His legacy isn't found in medals or decorations; it's found in the lives he touched. Ray planted strength, faith, and the courage to rise—not with arrogance, but with humility and heat. And that is what makes him not only a brother, but a blueprint for servant leadership.

My sister, **Jennifer, the Fearless Flame of Grace**, has always been bold—not the loud kind of bold, but the quiet, unshakable kind that holds families together and carries others through storms without asking for anything in return. For more than thirty years, she has served in healthcare as a Patient Service Representative—not just working a job but carrying out a mission. She is often the first face people see before a life-altering test, a scary diagnosis, or a long-awaited answer. And without fail, that face greets them with grace.

But make no mistake—grace doesn't mean weakness. Jennifer has always embodied a strength that is both gentle and fierce. She inherited our mother's Golden Rule and amplified it with her own brand of tenacity: "Always treat people the way you'd want to be treated—and if they forget, remind them without losing your own dignity." That's Jennifer.

She taught me how to laugh hard, love loud, and cry without apology. But above all, she taught me how to stand tall even when the world tries to knock me down. She's the one who reminded me to slow down, see people for who they are, and lead not just with authority, but with empathy. Her kind of leadership doesn't wear a title; it leaves an imprint. And in watching her, I didn't just learn how to lead —I learned how to live.

My wife, **Stephanie**, **the Architect of Alignment**, has been the steady pulse behind my progress. Analytical by nature and intentional in her support, she served as the quiet compass helping me stay true to my direction when the path shifted.

Through every relocation, every career pivot, and every season of uncertainty, she stood steady. While I was busy chasing elevation, she remained focused.

Her quiet strength reminded me that being different is not weakness—it is wisdom. Stephanie didn't just acknowledge the dream; she respected the discipline behind it.

The Bible says, "Two are better than one, because they have a good return for their labor" (Ecclesiastes 4:9). And in that way, she was a partner in the work, ensuring that progress was possible. For that, I remain grateful. Gratitude does not require sentiment—it requires honesty. And honestly, her presence has been a key part of the journey.

And so, to them—the roots of my becoming—I say this:

I carry your lessons and sacrifices not as burdens, but as wings.

Wings of love, faith, and legacy.

Because of you, I rise with purpose, I reach with courage, and I dare to become more than I ever imagined. But here's the thing—roots aren't glamorous. They don't pose for pictures. They don't beg for recognition. Yet, without them, nothing stands.

Without them, the rise is an illusion. My rise—any rise worth anything—is only as strong as what's underneath. And my foundation was deep, gritty, soaked in prayers, discipline, hard choices, and unwavering belief. My roots pushed through concrete, cracked generational limitations, and stretched through seasons of drought—only to bloom at the appointed time. And when the world saw the fruit, it didn't realize the battle it took underground.

That's where I was built.

And that's why I continue to HUSTLE—not for applause, but because my roots demand I grow toward purpose. Of course, there are many more who've supported me—too many to name. If I tried, this book would become about them! But they know who they are. And to each one, I say: "Thank you. May heaven smile upon you, bless your families, and bring to life every dream seeded in your spirit."

And with that, the transition began—not just in title, but in spirit. Not just in elevation, but in alignment.

KENNISM: Because of them, I've learned that real progress doesn't come from pushing alone—it comes from being pushed and pulled by love, legacy, and purpose.

Flourish isn't a fluke—it's the fruit of faithful roots. That's what this movement is built on.

That's why I continue to **Hustle While I Wait**.

Roots to My Rise

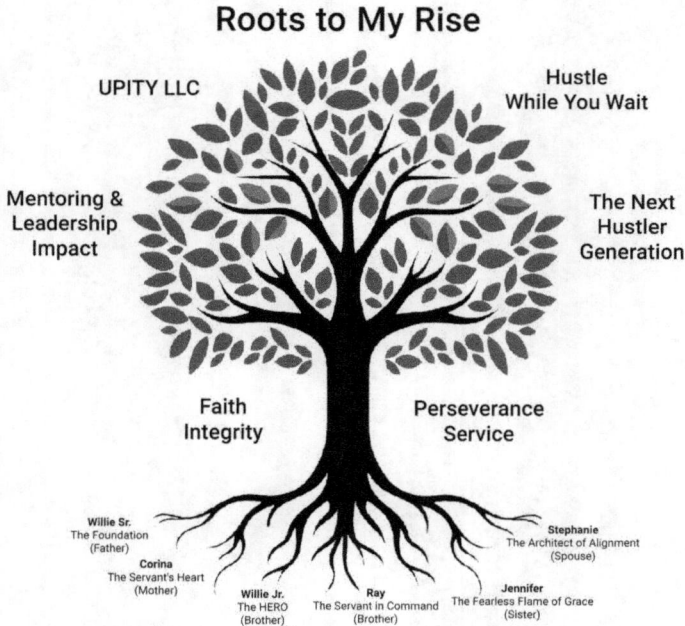

UPITY LLC

Hustle
While You Wait

Mentoring &
Leadership
Impact

The Next
Hustler
Generation

Faith
Integrity

Perseverance
Service

Willie Sr.
The Foundation
(Father)

Corina
The Servant's Heart
(Mother)

Willie Jr.
The HERO
(Brother)

Ray
The Servant in Command
(Brother)

Jennifer
The Fearless Flame of Grace
(Sister)

Stephanie
The Architect of Alignment
(Spouse)

The strength of my rise comes from the depth of my roots.
Every branch of my legacy draws from the faith and foundation planted
long before me.

Chapter 15

The Transition—How I Made the Shift, on My Terms

But one thing I do: Forgetting what is behind and straining toward what is ahead, I press on toward the goal to win the prize for which God has called me heavenward in Christ Jesus.

— Philippians 3:13–14

Empowerment

"I didn't walk away from a government career—I walked toward a calling."

There comes a point in your life when staying where you are costs more than moving forward. For me, that moment didn't arrive with fireworks or fanfare—it arrived with clarity. A quiet but undeniable truth: I wasn't just being called to do more; I was being called to become more.

I didn't walk away from a government career; I walked toward a calling. Nearly four decades of service had shaped me, sharpened me, and given me a platform. But a platform isn't the same as a purpose. This next chapter isn't about chasing success or running from a system—it's about ownership. Ownership of my gifts. Ownership of my growth. Ownership of a vision too large to fit inside the boundaries of a single career.

The voice inside me said, "You've served well. Now build something that carries your name, your values, and your vision." And that voice wasn't a whisper anymore—it was a charge.

I made the shift—not because it was easy, not because it was safe, but because it was time. I moved forward not with fear, but with faith. And most importantly, I redirected it with intention, knowing that the risk of standing still was far greater than the risk of stepping into the unknown. Many factors played a role in my transition—and yes, this might be my longest chapter yet, so hang in there with me.

This is more than a career move. This is legacy. Let me be clear: I didn't ask for permission—I answered the call.

FROM GOVERNMENT SERVICE TO UPITY

When I started at the agency thirty-nine years ago, it was all about me. My progress. My paycheck. My promotion. But over time, it stopped being about me and started being about the people I could support. Helping others move forward in their lives, their careers, and their purpose.

I had achieved what I set out to do nearly four decades ago: to lead as a Senior Executive in the federal government. You've already read about the road it took to get here—the intentional neglect, the moving goalposts, the 'not enough' that never seemed to end. But something shifted. The hunger that once drove me to prove myself had transformed into a calling to build something of my own.

Then came the Joint Duty Assignment. Leadership told me not to bother.

"You don't have the qualifications," they said.

"They want a Senior Executive, and you're only a GG-15."

My response? "Well, let them tell me no—just sign the paperwork, please!"

To their surprise, I got the interview. To their shock, I got the job. A position I couldn't even get an interview for at my own agency!

That moment confirmed what I already knew deep down: I could operate at the senior level. But the naysayers couldn't help themselves. "It's just temporary," they said. "You'll be back in a year."

My answer? So what? Temporary or not, I had already proven the point. I didn't need their stamp of approval—I had already stamped it myself.

When the door finally opened, it wasn't about validation. It was about peace. That's when I knew: It was time to move forward—not just on, but toward my next.

As my government career came to a close, I didn't see it as an ending. I saw it as a handoff—one season passing the baton to the next. My past wasn't disappearing. It was stepping aside so my future could take the lead.

For the first time, I felt the name UPITY not as a burden, but as a charge. A declaration. A call to rise higher, stand stronger, and walk fully in my purpose. The world outside wasn't waiting—it was wide open and calling my name.

And I answered. Not with fear—with clarity. Because purpose always pushes.

I'm no longer asking for permission. I'm making the call:

"It's time. No more waiting. No more excuses."

Ever heard of UPITY?

Let me introduce what's next.

UPITY—Unlimited Progress Integral To You—is more than a name.

It's not just a brand.

It's not just a business.

It's a movement.

Through UPITY LLC, I provide executive coaching, mentoring, and business/personal consultation. But beyond services, I deliver clarity, courage, and transformation—helping others rise, lead, and live without compromise.

This isn't just my next chapter. It's a blueprint for the next generation of leaders.

KENNISM: The road ahead feels uncertain—but for the first time in a long time, it also feels open. Full of possibility. Full of promise. And as I walked away from what no longer served me, I realized I wasn't leaving anything behind. I was making room for what's next. Government life was never meant to be forever—and that's OK. Some seasons are built to end. But I'm still here. And now, finally, I'm ready to rise. Because the next chapter? It's not just unwritten. **It's mine to create.**

CAREER JOURNEY TIMELINE
From Service to Significance

Early Federal Years
Learning the System

Strategic Impact Roles
Leading from the Middle

UPITY LLC & Beyond
Purpose in Motion

1986 — 1995 — 2005 — 2015 — 2025

Leadership Evolution

Becoming the Example

Began Mentoring Others

Launched M2M

Senior Leadership & Legacy Building

Hustling While Waiting

Balanced Purpose with Patience

Prepared for Transition

Every stage taught me to Hustle differently – not faster, but wiser

Chapter 16

Rules I Didn't Read, I Lived —Lessons I Learned the Hard Way, and Am Glad I Did

Let perseverance finish its work so that you may be mature and complete, not lacking anything.

—James 1:4

Wisdom

"The greatest lessons aren't in any rulebook—I had to live them to learn them. I didn't follow the rules—I followed the lessons. I didn't just read the book—I became the page."

- Sometimes it is as bad as you think. The challenge is how you'll deal with it.
- Whatever you do, always challenge yourself.
- The world will throw battles your way. But you get to choose which ones are worth the fight.
- Set a goal. Go get it.

- Make your own choices. And leave those alone who start with, "If I were you ...." Because they're not—YOU that is!
- In everything you do, do it like you're doing it for the Lord—not for people (Colossians 3:23).
- Don't know? Say "I don't know" and ask. Want to grow? Read. Reading is for the mind what weights are for the body—it builds strength.
- Success? You define it.
- Keep it real. Always.
- The question is not, "If I had ...," it's "Why didn't you?"

KENNISMS TO LIVE BY—AND FOR ANYONE WHO THOUGHT YOU WOULDN'T

These aren't just words—they're reminders, responses, and armor. Read them. Feel them. And when needed ... repeat them.

Intentional Neglect

"They ignored the seed—but they could never stop the root."

The Duck Mentality

"We're all ducks out here, doing our best to look cool while secretly paddling for our lives."

I Can See Now

"Real vision has more to do with my insight than my eyesight."

Is the Juice Worth the Squeeze

"Unless they wear a diaper, you can't change them."

The Onion Effect

"My tears are fertilizer. They grow things: grace, grit, and greatness."

Success Teaches You Nothing

"Success teaches you nothing—but failure teaches you everything."

'Cause You Let Me

"I can't complain if I let it happen."

Non-Negotiable

"Stay true. Stay grounded. Stay unmoved."

It Was Meant to Be Temporary

"Where you are going is bigger than where you have been."

Do What Is Sustainable

"Success that breaks you isn't success. True success builds you—mind, body, and spirit."

Here's What They Said

"Their words weren't just compliments—they were confirmations."

I Make No Apologies

"Make no apologies and be you. All others are taken."

The Roots of My Rise

"Flourish isn't a fluke—it's the fruit of faithful roots."

The Transition

"The next chapter isn't just unwritten—it's mine to create."

Rules I Didn't Read, I Lived

"I didn't read the rulebook—I wrote in my own margins."

Now It's Your Move

"In a world full of copycats, stay original. Be the lesson. Be the light."

KENNISM: These aren't rules from a handbook or leadership manual. I didn't read them—I lived them. Each one came from a real moment: a mistake, a breakthrough, or a decision that mattered. They've shaped how I lead, how I show up, and how I help others rise. And after all these years, they still hold. I'm passing them on—not as advice, but as truth earned in the trenches. Try them and see if they can work for you. I didn't skip the struggle—I studied it. I didn't read the rulebook—I wrote in my own margins. Trusting God wasn't my Plan B; it was the only way the plan made sense. In a world full of copycats, stay original. Be the lesson. Be the light. And never dim your shine just because they forgot their shades.

Now, before we close this journey, I want to leave you with something more than just words and lessons. Hustling while you wait isn't just strategy—it's soul work. And like all meaningful journeys, it deserves a benediction—a moment to reflect, honor, and be reminded of what truly matters in the wait.

A BENEDICTION FOR THE HUSTLE: A FINAL PRAYER OF FORGIVENESS AND THANKS

God, before I close this book, I pause not in weakness, but in worship.

I forgive them for the intentional neglect.

For seeing my effort but not my growth.

And I thank You that even when they ignored the seed, You kept watering it anyway.

(Philippians 1:6)

I forgive them for judging my journey by the surface—my suit, my smile, my silence.

And I thank You that beneath their chaos, You kept me calm, collected, and called.

(Psalm 37:7)

I forgive them for their backhanded compliments, their subtle sabotages, their low expectations.

And I thank You that their ceiling was never my limit. Their boundaries were not my border.

I forgive them for questioning my qualifications—for doubting my degrees, dismissing my deployment, and overlooking my leadership.

And I thank You that excellence needs no permission to shine. That I was already stamped with purpose.

(Philippians 1:6)

I forgive them for saying I was too sensitive—for mocking my tears and mistaking them for weakness.

And I thank You for every drop that watered my roots and helped me bloom with grace.

(Romans 12:21)

I forgive them for choosing silence when their voice could have made a difference.

And I thank You for being the loudest advocate in my quietest storms.

I forgive myself—for the times I believed them.

For shrinking. For overthinking. For hustling for their approval instead of honoring my own peace.

And I thank You—for the strength to keep showing up.

For the calling that wouldn't quit.

For the legacy rising, even when applause stayed silent.

This journey was not without its bruises—but every step was blessed.

I close this book not with bitterness, but with benediction.

Not with resentment, but with release.

Thank You for the Hustle.

Thank You for the Wait.

And thank You—that through it all—I never lost my Why.

Amen.

As I look back on everything I've shared—the lessons, the hustle, the moments in between—I realize that much of who I became started long before I ever held a title or walked into any office. It began with the word "UNIKUE" that my mother spoke over me ... a word that shaped my journey and still guides me today. Now, I bless the hustle—not for what it earned, but for what it revealed.

The truth is, you don't need anyone's permission to step into your calling. You already have it. The question now is simple:

What will you do with it?
The mirror is waiting.
The moment is now.
It's your move.

Let all that you do be done in love.

— 1 Corinthians 16:14

Chapter 17

Now It's Your Move— The Mirror Moment

Anyone who listens to the word but does not do what it says is like someone who looks at his face in a mirror and, after looking at himself, goes away and immediately forgets what he looks like. But whoever looks intently into the perfect law that gives freedom and continues in it—not forgetting what they have heard but doing it— they will be blessed in what they do.

—James 1:23–25

Action

"I took a deep breath and said, 'No more waiting. No more excuses.'"

KENNISM INTROSPECTION:

"Sometimes the road ahead isn't mapped out—but that doesn't mean you're lost. It just means you're free to build it yourself."

You've made it through the journey—not just mine, but your own. Every chapter you've read was more than a story. It was a mirror, a challenge, and an invitation. You've seen the highs and the lessons, the setbacks and the bounce-backs, the hustle and the hope.

Now, take a moment to breathe. Reflect. Reset. As a coach and lifelong learner of leadership, I leave you with a few questions to help you see your own reflection—to move from reading to doing, from observing to becoming (2 Corinthians 3:18).

- What did this book stir up in you that surprised you?
- What part of your story have you been waiting to tell—and what's stopping you?
- Who do you need to thank for being part of your hustle?
- What season in your life is coming to a close? What season is beginning?
- If you gave yourself permission to move, build, or believe, what would you do tomorrow?
- What does "your next" really look like?
- What legacy are you building—and who is watching you build it?

"Have I not commanded you? Be strong and courageous. Do not be afraid; do not be discouraged, for the Lord your God will be with you wherever you go."

—Joshua 1:9

Chapter 18

For the Next Hustler

Write the next move that fear has tried to talk you out of.

_____

_____

_____

_____

_____

_____

_____

_____

_____

_____

Endbook Review

THANK YOU FOR READING

If *Hustle While You Wait* encouraged you, challenged you, or helped you see your journey with new clarity, I'd like to ask one final favor.

Please consider leaving a brief, honest review on **Amazon**.

Your review helps other readers discover this book at the exact moment they may need it most.

You don't need to write anything long or polished.

A few sentences are enough.

You might share:

• What stood out to you most

• How the book resonated with your current season

• Who you'd recommend it to

If you would like to stay connected with Kenneth LeGrand and explore additional insights, resources, and updates related to his work, you can visit his author website at **kenlegrandauthor.com**. There you'll find information about his books, mentorship work, and ongoing guidance designed to help readers remain focused, patient, and purposeful during seasons of preparation.

Thank you again for taking this journey through *Hustle While You Wait*. Stay encouraged, stay committed to the process, and continue building toward the opportunities ahead.

Recommended Reading: Resources for the Hustle

These works have shaped how I think about leadership, legacy, and the power of purpose. They challenge, sharpen, and sustain the Hustle—even in the waiting seasons.

Leadership & Purpose Uncommon

- John C. Maxwell—*The 21 Irrefutable Laws of Leadership* (Thomas Nelson, 1998)
- Brené Brown—*Dare to Lead: Brave Work. Tough Conversations*. Whole Hearts. (Random House, 2018)
- Daniel Goleman—*Working with Emotional Intelligence* (Bantam Books, 1998)
- Adam Grant—*Give and Take: Why Helping Others Drives Our Success* (Viking, 2013)
- Greg McKeown—*Essentialism: The Disciplined Pursuit of Less* (Crown Currency, 2014)

Emotional Resilience & Renewal

- Christina Maslach & Michael Leiter—*The Truth About Burnout* (Jossey-Bass, 1997)

- Daniel Kahneman—*Thinking, Fast and Slow* (Farrar, Straus, and Giroux, 2011)
- Walter Mischel—*The Marshmallow Test: Understanding Self-Control* (Little, Brown, 2014)
- Harvard Business Review—*Manage Your Energy, Not Your Time* (Schwartz & McCarthy, 2007)
- Harvard Business Review—*The Best Leaders Are Humble Leaders* (Prime & Salib, 2014)

Faith, Character & Integrity

- Dean Alfange—*My Creed* (originally published in Reader's Digest, 1952)
- Carl Rogers—*On Becoming a Person: A Therapist's View of Psychotherapy* (Houghton Mifflin, 1961)
- William Shakespeare—*Hamlet* & *King Henry IV (Part II)*
- The Holy Bible—Proverbs 27:2; Ecclesiastes 9:11; Isaiah 49:1

For Reflection & Renewal

- Earl Nightingale—*The Strangest Secret* (1956)
- Harvard Business Review—*The Restorative Power of Small Habits* (Mereu & Jordan, 2024)
- Johns Hopkins Medicine—*Forgiveness: Your Health Depends on It* (Wellness & Prevention Article)

These books and studies aren't just resources—they're reminders that the pursuit of leadership is lifelong. Read them not to repeat what's been said, but to recognize the truth in your own story.

References

Alfange, Dean. 1952. "My Creed." Reader's Digest, October.

Ashkenas, Ron. 2016. "Even Experienced Executives Avoid Conflict." *Harvard Business Review*, March 8, 2016. https://hbr.org/2016/03/even-experienced-executives-avoid-conflict

Carucci, Ron. 2024. "5 Ways New Leaders (Accidentally) Erode Trust on Their Teams." *Harvard Business Review*, March 18, 2024. https://hbr.org/2024/03/5-ways-new-leaders-accidentally-erode-trust-on-their-teams

Fox, Glenn R., Jonas Kaplan, Hanna Damasio, and Antonio Damasio. 2015. "Neural Correlates of Gratitude." *Frontiers in Psychology* 6 (September): 1491. https://doi.org/10.3389/fpsyg.2015.01491

Goleman, Daniel. 1998. "Working with Emotional Intelligence." Bantam Books.

Goleman, Daniel. 2000. "Leadership that Gets Results." *Harvard Business Review*, March–April 2000. https://hbr.org/2000/03/leadership-that-gets-results

Grant, Adam. 2013. "Give and Take: Why Helping Others Drives Our Success." Viking.

Harvard Business Review. 2025. "Misconceptions That Undermine Psychological Safety." April 23, 2025. https://hbr.org/tip/2025/04/misconceptions-that-undermine-psychological-safety

Johns Hopkins Medicine. n.d. "Forgiveness: Your Health Depends on It." https://www.hopkinsmedicine.org/health/wellness-and-prevention/forgiveness-your-health-depends-on-it

Kahneman, Daniel. 2011. "Thinking, Fast and Slow." Farrar, Straus, and Giroux.

Kyeong, Sunghyon, Joohan Kim, Dae Jin Kim, Hesun Erin Kim, and Jae-Jin Kim. 2017. "Effects of Gratitude Meditation on Neural Network Functional Connectivity and Brain-Heart Coupling." *Scientific Reports* 7 (1): 5058. https://doi.org/10.1038/s41598-017-05520-9

Maslach, Christina, and Leiter, Michael P. 1997. "The Truth About Burnout: How Organizations Cause Personal Stress and What to Do About It." Jossey-Bass.

Maxwell, John C. 1998. "The 21 Irrefutable Laws of Leadership." Thomas Nelson.

McKeown, Greg. 2014. "Essentialism: The Disciplined Pursuit of Less." Crown Currency.

Mereu, Francesca Giulia, and Jennifer Jordan. 2024. "The Restorative Power of Small Habits." *Harvard Business Review*, February 9, 2024. https://hbr.org/2024/02/the-restorative-power-of-small-habits

Mischel, Walter, and Ebbe B. Ebbesen. 1970. "Attention in Delay of Gratification." *Journal of Personality and Social Psychology*, 16 (2): 329–337. https://doi.org/10.1037/h0029815

Prime, Jeanine, and Elizabeth Salib. 2014. "The Best Leaders Are Humble Leaders." *Harvard Business Review*, May 12, 2014. https://hbr.org/2014/05/the-best-leaders-are-humble-leaders

Rogers, Carl. 1961. "On Becoming a Person: A Therapist's View of Psychotherapy." Houghton Mifflin.

Schwartz, Tony, and Catherine McCarthy. 2007. "Manage Your Energy, Not Your Time." *Harvard Business Review*, October 1, 2007. https://hbr.org/2007/10/manage-your-energy-not-your-time

Shakespeare, William. 1597. "King Henry IV, Part II: Act 3, Scene 1."

Shakespeare, William. 1600. "Hamlet, Prince of Denmark: Act 1, Scene 3."

Taylor, Tate, dir. 2011. "The Help." DreamWorks Pictures.

Thorndike, Edward L. 1920. "A Constant Error in Psychological Ratings." *Journal of Applied Psychology*, 4 (1): 25–29. https://doi.org/10.1037/h0071663

Watts, Tyler W., Greg J. Duncan, and Haonan Quan. 2018. "Revisiting the Marshmallow Test: A Conceptual Replication Investigating Links Between Early Delay of Gratification and Later Outcomes." *Psychological Science* 29 (7): 1159–77. https://doi.org/10.1177/0956797618761661

All references listed above are cited directly or thematically referenced within the manuscript. They provide academic, literary, and cultural grounding to the core leadership principles discussed in *Hustle While You Wait*.

www.ingramcontent.com/pod-product-compliance
Lightning Source LLC
La Vergne TN
LVHW051247080426
835513LV00016B/1795